BEVERLEY MINSTER

Historical text by
Professor David Palliser

A Welcome from the Vicar

Welcome to Beverley Minster. The towering splendour of the minster dominates the horizon for many miles. Its architecture not only delights the eye, but also conveys aspects of the Christian gospel that is the reason for its existence. Its towers, rising heavenwards from the soil of East Yorkshire, point to God, Creator and Father, who is above us and beyond us, yet has planted His footsteps on earth. Its cruciform shape represents the cross of Jesus Christ which is at the very heart of Christian faith. The spaciousness of its interior and the ability of its features to catch the visitor by surprise evoke the freedom and unpredictability of the Holy Spirit who dwells within Christians and brings them to life. It is no wonder, then, that so many visitors comment on a remarkable spiritual atmosphere within the building as well as its physical beauty.

We pray that you also will experience here something of the presence of the Christian God, Father, Son and Holy Spirit, who is able to bring new purpose and hope in life.

Although the word 'minster' is a translation of the Latin word monasterium, meaning 'monastery', in Anglo-Saxon times it was also used to mean any large church served by a body of priests. The term is still popularly used for other great churches which had cathedral or college status, such as York, Lincoln, Ripon and Southwell.

Beverley Minster is built on the scale of a cathedral, and it is in the view of many architectural writers finer than some churches which are cathedrals: for instance, it has been judged by Alec Clifton-Taylor 'the finest non-cathedral church in the kingdom' after Westminster Abbey.

Many visitors are surprised to find such a magnificent building in a small town like Beverley, but the reasons are simple: Beverley was not a small town by medieval standards. Most of the church we see today was built between 1220 and 1400, and it was during that period (in 1377) that Beverley was taxed as the eleventh largest town in England. The minster was not a mere parish church but a wealthy collegiate church and a centre for pilgrims.

It had been founded for monks, but from the 10th to the 16th centuries it was staffed by a regulated group of priests who served the town and the surrounding area. In 1548 the Crown seized most of the minster's revenues, in a suppression of colleges comparable to the dissolution of the monasteries, and reduced it to the status of a parish church. Neglect of the fabric through lack of funds nearly caused disaster, but fortunately major restorations since the 18th century have saved it, and it still stands today, combining its parochial functions with being effectively, as it was intended, a sub-cathedral in the large diocese of York.

ABOVE: *A bagpiper, one of the minster's fine Decorated label stops.* ㉑

LEFT: *A panel from the great west window depicting the synod of Arles in* AD *314.* ㉕

RIGHT: *The choir. Beyond the high altar is the Perpendicular great east window (c.1417).* ⑩

INTRODUCTION

We know very little about the origins of Beverley and its minster except for what St Bede tells us in his *Ecclesiastical History of the English People* (AD 731). There is evidence of Roman and prehistoric settlement in the area, but St Bede implies that the district was uninhabited when Bishop John of York (706–*c.*714) founded a monastery there. Almost certainly this stood on the site of the minster; the site of the black marble slab in front of the nave was always regarded as his original tomb, and was in the Middle Ages a focus for pilgrims and for miracles of healing. Nothing is known of John's church and little certain known of the minster for 300 years after his death. Later traditions spoke of a sack by the Vikings, and of the church's refoundation as a college of canons by King Athelstan (924–39).

However, we do know that Archbishop Aelfric secured John's canonization as St John of Beverley in 1037, and that he and his successors enlarged and decorated the church: Archbishop Ealdred, who crowned William the Conqueror, built a new presbytery (choir) which may have been modelled on Westminster Abbey, making it the earliest 'Norman' church in northern England. So many pilgrims flocked to John's tomb that a flourishing market town grew up on the north side of the church.

By the 12th century the church had the wealth and status that it retained right through to the Reformation: the Archbishop of York was lord of the town, but the minster was controlled by a provost and seven (later eight) canons, who enjoyed great wealth, particularly from a generous royal grant of corn. The church's privileges included sanctuary rights for fugitives, not only within the church but throughout the town, and the remains of three sanctuary crosses still stand alongside roads leading into Beverley, marking the outer limits of those rights.

The minster also housed the banner of St John, which was credited with the power to grant victory in battle, and which was frequently borrowed by kings to this end. Edward I did so, for example, on his Scottish campaigns, and made generous gifts to the minster in return. Later, John's cult received a further boost when Henry V won the battle of Agincourt (1415) on one of his feast days, and made John one of the patron saints of the Royal Family.

ABOVE: *A primitive 17th-century painting, depicting King Athelstan handing St John a charter of privileges – a charming yet historically impossible scene.* ⑯

LEFT AND RIGHT: *Lead figures of King Athelstan (left) and St John of Beverley, dating from 1781, which form a pair in the nave south aisle.* ㉓

It is likely that the minster continued to be rebuilt in the new Norman style between the 1060s and 1170s; certainly it retains its Norman font as well as much re-used Norman stone. But in 1188 a fire badly damaged the church, and in about 1213 the central tower collapsed.

The present church was begun in the Early English style, it is thought in the 1220s. Building started at the east end and proceeded rapidly, the first bay of the nave being completed by about 1260–70. St John's relics were transferred to a new shrine behind the high altar soon after 1300, and the beautiful reredos (stone screen) was built to carry it.

By 1311 work had restarted on the nave, in an adapted Early English style rather than the Decorated style by that time in fashion. This stroke of genius makes the building a harmonious whole, especially when viewed from inside. The nave was completed only in the 1390s, the western towers and north porch being added soon after 1400 in the Perpendicular style. No attempt was made to build a new central tower, presumably because of the spongy ground and the problem of foundations. The medieval church was now virtually complete.

In 1548 the college of canons was suppressed, and the government seized most of the church revenues. The Chapter House was demolished, and the whole fabric became badly neglected. Fortunately Nicholas Hawksmoor carried out a major

LEFT: *Part of the north-west window depicting St Augustine of Canterbury.* ㉖

RIGHT: *The great west door, with effigies of the Four Evangelists: left to right, John, Luke, Mark and Matthew.* ㉕

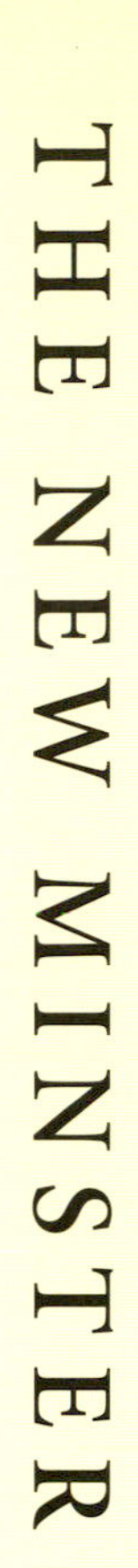

restoration between 1717 and 1731, and his collaborator, William Thornton, literally saved the north transept from collapse. Another major restoration was carried out by Sir George Gilbert Scott between 1866 and 1878, and Canon Nolloth (Vicar 1880–1921) installed many new furnishings including stained-glass windows, bells, many exterior statues and the wrought-iron railings around the churchyard. These works, together with a further restoration in 1975–86 and new furnishings, have put the minster in good repair to continue to serve future generations.

ABOVE: *The treadwheel crane, used to winch materials through the crossing ceiling.* ⑮

RIGHT: *Toothache – a label stop.* ㉑

Ideally, a tour of the minster should begin outside, starting with the earliest parts at the east end and working in a clockwise direction. On the south side the harmonious blend of styles – Early English eastern arm, Decorated nave and Perpendicular western towers – is seen to best advantage. The earliest stonework is of local oolitic limestone, but the bulk of the building is of magnesian limestone from the Tadcaster area, and fortunately the Georgian restorers had access to second-hand supplies of the same stone (from St Mary's Abbey, York). Unusually, however, much of the external stone at Beverley is original.

The exterior reveals the cathedral scale of the building. It is about 111 metres (365 feet) long externally, and it has double transepts copied (like much else in the 13th-century parts) from Lincoln. All that is lacking for the complete Gothic scheme is a proper central tower: the present very low one was added by Hawksmoor in 1721, replacing a dome.

The many flying buttresses were necessary to carry the thrust of the stone vaults down to the ground. The details of doors, windows, buttresses, parapets, gables and turrets are worth studying, including the rose windows of the main transepts, and the worn sculptures on the parapets of the nave aisles. Three medieval statues survive on the exterior: St John and King Athelstan on either side of the great east window, and a man in armour, said to represent Henry Percy, 1st Earl of Northumberland, just above Queen Victoria on the north-west tower. Remains of the church of St Martin, once a separate parish church, can be seen between the two sundials at the south-west corner of the church. Finally, the west front with its twin towers is superb.

ABOVE: The imposing early 15th-century Highgate porch. ㉗

LEFT: The principal doorway to the south transept, like the rest of the magnificent façade, is pure Early English. ⑲

RIGHT: A statue, said to be of Henry Percy, 1st Earl of Northumberland, on the north-west tower.

THE BELLS
The north tower houses a peal of ten bells, cast by Taylors of Loughborough in 1901; in the south tower are 'Great John' (another Taylors' bell of 1901) and two medieval bells, 'Peter' (currently used as the prayer bell) and 'Brithunus'.

The medieval minster was surrounded by other buildings forming a close – the Chapter House, dormitory, refectory, canons' houses, and so on – but none of them survive any longer except, perhaps, embedded in some of the older houses in St John Street. Hall Garth, the open field south of the nave, is the site of the palace which was used by the medieval archbishops of York when they stayed in Beverley.

The usual entrance is through the two-storeyed Highgate porch, added in the early 15th century to make an imposing entrance from the town.

Nearly a century ago, the architectural historian Joseph Morris claimed that 'Beverley Minster may fairly be reckoned the most beautiful building in Yorkshire', superior to York Minster 'in almost everything save mere bulk and mere first-sight impressiveness.' That is a judgement with which many will agree, especially once they have viewed the interior with its unity of style, its satisfying proportions and its exquisite details.

The pattern is set by the older, eastern parts, including the choir and both pairs of transepts: all is in a pure, Early English style similar to Lincoln and Salisbury cathedrals, with lancet windows, 'dog-tooth' decoration, stiff-leaf capitals, and colonettes of dark, polished Purbeck marble contrasting with the stonework; the whole is crowned by a vaulted roof. Recent research has showed that the beauty of the overall design is no accident; the medieval designers employed a very coherent system of measurements, though the technicalities need not be grasped to appreciate the results. Among other things, the roof is made to seem even higher than it is because of the slender proportions: the vault is 30 metres (100 feet) high, but the chancel and main transepts are only 8 metres (27 feet) wide. Such proportions are close to those of the Gothic cathedrals of France, and as Christopher Wilson puts it, 'although direct French influences are unlikely, Beverley comes nearer than any other example of the Early English style to the . . . beauty of Soissons or Amiens.'

Whether because of this beauty, or a simple conservative respect for the past, the 14th-century builders of the nave chose to continue the system of the eastern parts with the very minimum of changes. Purbeck marble was almost completely abandoned, and window tracery and capitals of columns adopted the new Decorated style, but the overall effect, which must have been deliberate, is one of unity. No other major church, except Westminster Abbey two generations later, was so conservative in its stylistic continuity. It is this feature above all which makes Beverley Minster, though it took two centuries to complete, a single harmonious whole.

ABOVE: *A capital depicting St John and King Athelstan.* ⑤

LEFT: *The Norman font of Frosterley marble, with its splendid wooden cover (1726) carved by the Thorntons.* ㉔

RIGHT: *The nave, looking east.* ㉕

THE INTERIOR

Like all the eastern parts of the minster, the retrochoir – the area behind the high altar – is in the Early English style, characterized by pointed arches, lancet windows, stiff-leaf foliage capitals, and many columns of dark, polished Purbeck marble from Dorset.

The 14th-century reredos has beautiful patterned carving and figure sculpture, including musicians. Medieval and Tudor graffiti here probably date from the time when the retrochoir was used as a grammar school. On the side facing the choir, the reredos was largely renewed in 1826, and covered with statues and mosaics in 1897.

The great east window, inserted shortly after 1416, now includes most of the medieval stained glass which survived the Reformation. The lower part includes 21 small scenes of 13th-century date, depicting episodes from the lives of St Martin, St Nicholas, and possibly St Leonard. Other glass, including the large figures in the lower half, is 14th century, while the upper half of the window retains much of the original glass of *c.*1416–20. The retrochoir also houses some fine monuments of the 17th to 19th centuries, mostly of members of the local families of Warton and Pennyman.

ABOVE: *The north choir aisle. The double stair once led to an octagonal Chapter House, demolished in 1550.* ⑨

TOP RIGHT: *The high altar.* ⑧

ABOVE: *The Percy tomb, with (top left) its Decorated freestone canopy, is a crowning achievement of medieval European art.* ⑥

Off the north choir aisle is the Northumberland Chapel, added to house the tomb of Henry Percy, 4th Earl of Northumberland, who was murdered by rebels in 1489. The Percys were the dominant local aristocrats in the 14th and 15th centuries, living nearby at Leconfield. A little further west stands another Percy tomb, possibly that of Lady Eleanor Percy, who died in 1328. What is certain, however, is that this is the finest surviving British tomb of its time.

Between the reredos and the Percy Tomb stands the oldest surviving object in the minster, known as the Frith Stool. It is traditionally linked to the minster's right of sanctuary (*frithu* is the Anglo-Saxon word for 'peace'), but may have been originally a bishop's or abbot's throne.

The best feature of the north choir aisle is the double staircase which once led to the doors of the demolished chapter house. Opposite this is a list of the provosts, vicars and organists of the minster; one famous name included, though he never lived in Beverley, is Thomas Becket, Provost *c.*1153–62, who later became the archbishop of Canterbury, saint and martyr.

ABOVE: *The Frith Stool or Chair of Peace, probably an Anglo-Saxon bishop's or abbot's throne.* ⑦

ABOVE: *A boss on the reredos depicting the Coronation of the Blessed Virgin Mary.* ①

In the chancel, the minster's Early English architecture is seen in all its glory with its three storeys – arcades, triforium and clerestory – crowned by a stone vault. The 13th-century designers must have enjoyed playing with patterns and shapes: for example, the blank arcading in the triforium is doubled to create a 'syncopated' rhythm, and the four great piers of the east crossing (above the high altar) overhang at the top. Above this, but visible only from the roof, are traces of what may have been an abandoned attempt to build an eastern tower.

Altogether the choir is full of good furnishings, including 14th-century wooden sedilia (the seats to the south of the altar), 18th-century marble flooring with a *trompe l'oeil* (deceives the eye) pattern, and Victorian ceiling paintings by Scott in the style of the 13th century. The sedilia cleverly echo the nodding arches of the Percy Tomb opposite, and may well have been designed by the same hand. Best of all are the choirstalls, constructed in about 1520. The oak canopies, with their tiny vaults, have been much restored, and some of the heads and figures on canopies and bench-ends are Georgian or Victorian; but the medieval bench-ends include a fine elephant and castle (perhaps representing Queen Catherine of Aragon?) on the south side. Underneath the seats are 68 misericords (carved scenes on tip-up seats), more than in any English cathedral. Unfortunately, the seats are now fragile and permission is needed to view them, but they are notable for their portrayal of very realistic animals, with domestic and farmyard scenes. The choir is terminated to the west by the organ and organ screen, but these are better viewed from the nave.

LEFT: *The choir, looking west, with its* trompe l'oeil *Georgian flooring.* ⑩

LEFT: *One of the minster's 68 fine misericords with, left, its supporter enlarged.* ⑩

Both transepts are spacious, each with two aisles, and their architecture is beautifully restrained Early English. In the early years of the 18th century, the north transept was on the point of collapse when William Thornton of York pushed the north wall back into place with a giant wooden frame; even today the north-east pillar has a visible lean.

The finest monument in the north transept is the priest's tomb, almost certainly that of Provost Nicholas de Huggate (died 1338). His effigy is beautifully carved with mass vestments decorated with heraldic shields, which helped to identify him; the tomb chest may well be from another monument, probably the tomb canopy in the nave.

The crossing space is usually occupied by the circular movable altar (1970), and this partly covers another fine 18th-century pavement. The intricate wooden screen of 1878–80 was designed by Scott to match the choirstalls, and was carved by James Elwell of Beverley. It is surmounted by Johann Snetzler's superb organ of 1769, housed in a case of 1916 designed by Arthur Hill. Thanks to sympathetic repair and restoration over the years it retains more Snetzler pipework than any other organ.

In the ceiling directly above the nave altar is a circular boss in richly painted wood; this is removable, to allow building materials to be hoisted into the tower. The massive treadwheel which used to operate the hoist can still be seen in the roof.

The south transept, though architecturally fine, has few outstanding furnishings except for the military memorials in the eastern chapels. The central chapel has a cenotaph (which was designed by F.L. Pearson in 1921) commemorating the men of the East Yorkshire Regiment who died in the First World War, and modelled on the tomb of King Edward the Confessor in Westminster Abbey, while in the other chapels hang old colours of the regiment.

ABOVE: *A monument in memory of Major General Bowes (died 1812) with artillery and an angel writing his epitaph.* ⑰

ABOVE: *St Michael overcoming the Devil, a panel from the north transept north window.* ⑬

RIGHT: *The choir screen, designed by Scott and made by James Elwell of Beverley.* ⑭

The floor slab marking the tomb of St John represents the very origin of minster and town. From here one can study the transition from the first bay of the nave to the later work further west; the general style and proportions remained unchanged, though the nave windows are in the new Decorated style (and Perpendicular further west), and in the north aisle the wall arcading is in full 14th-century style. Nevertheless, such respect for a style of the past is rare among the greater English medieval churches. The vault is no longer of stone but of brick, a remarkable early use of such a material in England.

The nave and nave aisles have their fair share of interesting features. Perhaps the most exquisite are the carvings of men, women and angels playing musical instruments, above the nave pillars and along the north aisle. Altogether in the minster there are over 70 of these – more, it is said, than in any other European church, but no one knows why.

The earliest features of the nave are the Norman font, a huge piece of Frosterley marble from County Durham, and, a little further east, a 14th-century tomb canopy traditionally called the 'two sisters' tomb', though it is not known who is buried there. However, the best furnishings are Georgian and Victorian, an especially interesting combination as in most churches the Victorians obliterated the Georgian fittings. To some extent this happened at Beverley too – the Georgian pews, galleries and choir screen were all removed, though the two splendid painted lead figures of John and Athelstan from the choir screen were spared, and now stand on either side of the nave south doors. Much Georgian woodwork also remains, in particular the south and west doors and the font cover.

The Victorian and Edwardian restorers contributed to the nave, the brass lectern, the stone statues at the west end, and a fine set of stained-glass windows, most of them by the firms of Hardman & Co, and Clayton & Bell.

ABOVE: *The Crucifixion, from a window in the south transept.* ⑲

LEFT: *The nave is 14th-century, except for the nearest bay with its lavish use of black Purbeck marble. In the centre foreground is the tomb of St John.* ⑳

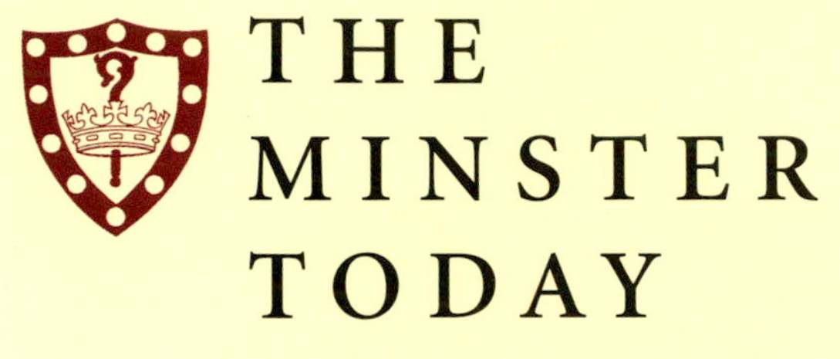

THE MINSTER TODAY

A Postscript by the Vicar

For many centuries, a vision of the glory of God and of Christian service towards the local community has inspired the generations of clergy and lay people associated with Beverley Minster. Today, at the very beginning of the third Christian millennium, this vision is held as strongly as it has ever been, as the minster seeks to fulfil its role both as parish church to some 17,000 of Beverley's townspeople and also as a focus for faith and community life in the wider region of East Yorkshire.

In today's diverse society, the minster offers a wide range of styles of worship in a monthly pattern, which includes informal services and services for all ages worshipping together, alongside the more traditional worship of the Church of England. Many people come seeking God's involvement with them at critical times in their lives through baptisms, weddings and funerals, and others make use of St Katherine's Chapel for private prayer. Special services of thanksgiving or remembrance are held throughout the year.

The minster's place in the community has been strengthened in recent years with the appointment of a full-time youth leader who is particularly active in the schools of the parish. Young people play a big part in the church alongside the large number of adult townsfolk who offer their time and abilities to those activities, often hidden from view, which make up its regular life. The 'Friends of Beverley Minster' organization unites all those throughout the world who wish to be associated with its work.

Through prayer and action, Beverley Minster continues to bring the grace and peace of Jesus Christ to many people. We trust that it will bring blessing to you.